Raw Spirit

by,
Angela Taylor Perry

Inner Intimacies of the Soul

Copyright © 2011 by Angela Taylor Perry. 69928-TAYL

ISBN: Softcover 978-1-4653-9498-9

All rights reserved. No part of this book may be reproduced or transmitted in any form or by any means, electronic or mechanical, including photocopying, recording, or by any information storage and retrieval system, without permission in writing from the copyright owner.

To order additional copies of this book, contact:
Xlibris Corporation
1-888-795-4274
www.Xlibris.com
Orders@Xlibris.com

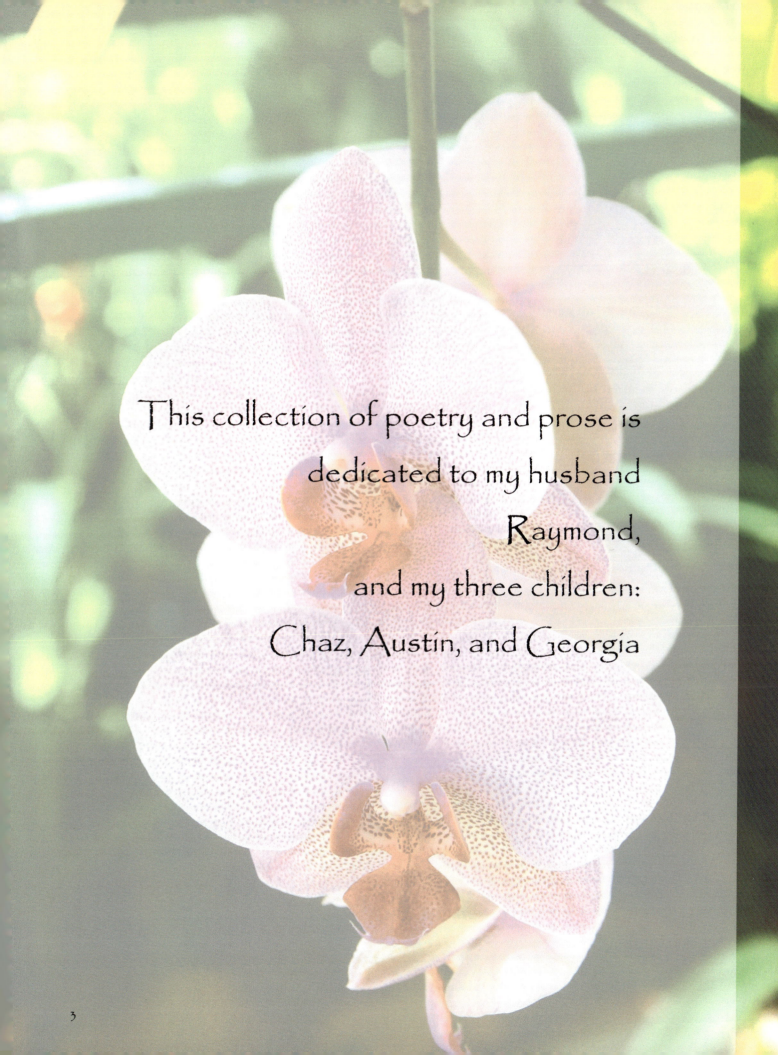

This collection of poetry and prose is
dedicated to my husband
Raymond,
and my three children:
Chaz, Austin, and Georgia

RAW SPIRIT

Acknowledgments

Giving honor to my Lord & Savior Jesus Christ who is the head of my life, my best friend & husband Raymond, Our children, Chaz, Austin, Georgia, Minielle & Marva. My great-grandmother Georgia, my mother's Edna & Roberta, my father's Ambrose & Charles, my sisters: Candy, Linda, Ava, & Gretchen Jerri Smith, Blanche Patterson, Nancy Dorner, Buddy Hannah, Gwen Etter-Lewis, Stacey Salters, George Opdyke, Diann Lentz, Sharon Hill, Consuela Walker, Willie Mae Pierson, ZoeAnn Chavous, Hamidah Shabazz, Carlos Worthy, Elizabeth McCracklin, Deborah Warfield, Joy Ray, Sharon Wysinger, Johnnie Collins, Betty Lindsey, Peggy Lee, Cheryl Carr, Lynette White, Anita Walker, Joseph & Patricia Sobota, Judy Scott, Cheryl Joseph, Sandra Weeden, Bessie Jackson, Ryan & Joy Bailey, Drew & Jackie Busch, John Witvliet, Ruth Tucker, Brenda DeKam, and especially Vickie Pickett-Patterson.

Allow yourself to grow with me in finding the inner joy and peace
in what God has created in you...

"I will praise thee for I am fearfully and wonderfully made"
Psalm 139:14

Introduction

Some folk find my testimony
my willingness to suffer
my confession
my submission to claiming Multiple Sclerosis as a gift
my not be willing to change a moment of my fight
unbelievable, humiliating
impossible, unnecessary

Some folk listen to my confession
with pity in their eyes
and deep sorrow in their voices
this poor beautiful soul
she doesn't deserve such hardship

Some folk shake their heads
in the midst of God's grace
with encouraging responses
words of empathy, they think

I say
I come to you not as a model for enduring physical
and mental affliction
no
I come to you as a broken living vessel of God's grace
a conduit of God's love and forgiveness
his healing power
I expose my inner self to you so that you can see
the work of the Cross
so that you may know
that Christ carried the cross for all
confessing hearts

RAW SPIRIT

Messy Spirituality

"God hath chosen the foolish things of the world to confound the wise and God hath chosen the weak things of the world to confound the things which are mighty; that no man's flesh should glory in his presence"
1 Corinthians 1:27, 29

"Silence reminds me to take my soul with me wherever I go."

Detachment...
"Being free from wanting certain things to happen and remaining so trusting of God that "what is happening will be the thing you want and you will be at peace with it all."
-Karen Norris-

The more I turn to God and ask Him to use me for His purposes, the more my mind expands and illumines. I experience the peace of God more deeply and the joy of my natural innocense more often as I learn to apply this concept of "detachment".

A more personal definition of detachment for me is a spiritual commitment to make every situation an object of spiritual connection. When I can honestly do this, something miraculous happens. First, I begin to experience an *'out of the ordinary phenomena'*. Somewhere between the fear of being in front of people and the discomfort of multiple sclerosis; while singing I am lifted up beyond it all. I experience a sensational manifestation of healing that leaves me with no physical awareness of my pain. It feels as though my mind expands, and my emotional abilities become sharpened and level-headed. I feel centered in my strengths, as though I have entered a gulf-stream of spiritual ecstasy and joy.

In this state there is an acute consciousness that I am capable and while in this "new creature" moment Spirit integrates its supreme confidence miraculously throughout my body. It is joyful to be in this state because by His grace I have broken through barriers which normally hold me back. I am standing firm within the resurrected power of his love.

I believe that the practice of monastic silence is a key to maintaining this level of spiritual consciousness. Practicing silence in God's presence forces me to trash all personal fancies and become conscious of the presence of God. Silence forces me to realize that it is God who gives me the freedom to detach myself from my pain. It is God who helps me accept the reality of my being "born again" with courage to shout about it to all who will listen.

Allelujah!

Messy Spirituality
Michael Yaconelli

Yaconelli celebrates that,
"Spirituality is not a formula; it is not a test. It is a relationship.
spirituality is not about competency; it is about intimacy.
spirituality is not about perfection; it is about connection.
spiritual life begins where we are <u>now</u> in the mess of our lives.
accepting the reality of our broken,
flawed lives is the beginning of spirituality
not because the spiritual life will remove our flaws
but because we *let go* of seeking perfection and,
instead, seek God." (p.13)

I have spent most of my life comparing myself with other imperfect human beings.
I have degraded myself with thoughts that
I am too short, too fat, not smart enough,
and not pretty enough.
This book is helping me to celebrate
that I am not perfect and
that is what's great!

Becoming Beautiful

As a teenager my vision of becoming beautiful was a tall, hour glass figure with long flowing brown hair. As a child of God I am discovering daily that *beauty* is God's inner calm spirit within me. It is his radiance of strength and love that makes me beautiful.

This is a profound statement for woman who has spent years searching for love from outward adornment and flattering lips. By the time I reached my early thirties, I had convinced myself that I had no self-esteem. It was self-worth I was missing. I had no concept of my personal and private rights. The results of verbal, physical and sexual abuse defined the inner torment in my soul. Fear, and procrastination were my silent middle names.

Glory be to God! He has given me an extra measure of courage to risk vulnerability and disclose my journey towards wholeness.
My decision to become a Christian washed away every wrongful act.
Truly I am a new creature! It is my prayer that those who see fulfillment in Christ will be challenged, changed, and convicted to live a life devoted to Truth.

When I began my spiritual journey
I was in great turmoil over a
man
I was unhappy
and lonely
I asked God for peace of mind
I didn't ask him to change the
circumstance
just for peace
he gave me what I asked for
he gave me
Himself...

I Like Me

You know sometime
like this time
I really like me
I like me when I am into me!
not feeling disoriented
and fractured because
he is not here or
not there or in me
but really, I like me now
because I feel Him inside me
like a rushing wind
like a beautiful waterfall
and I smile
I hear birds
all kinds
whispering in my ear
and I smile
I feel love
down to my toes
I know this love
love that sets
fire to desire
and I smile
I take flight to explore
the inner intimacies
of my soul
my heart
my mind
I am complete
in these thoughts
of liking me
Psalm 139: 14

Today

This has been an interesting day
Full of love. . . laughter
a complete day accept
for a little mental disorganization
woke up depressed
thinking about all of them
Him in my spirit
him in my heart
her in my psyche
then there is me. . .
I think?
Maybe it's anesthetic
the way I think in the morning
residue from old dreams
and faded faces
maybe it's the fantasy line I play
wishing for the Butler
to help me with my bath
and Missy the maid to bring me
cream and strawberries
Maybe it's lost lavish thoughts of lust
pleasures and all their
damned directed erections
to get there
There is so much to wake up to
but what to do first?
Suddenly I realize I can do anything
I am in charge of me
I start to get excited
but I want it all
but what first?
who first? Him. . .
him. . .
or her?

RAW SPIRIT

***I now realize that my spiritual growth over 30 years is not because my brokenness or my flaws have been removed. The brokenness in my life has spiritually formed me. This is good news! Scripture teaches that I can count it all joy when I go through trials and temptations because through them I am more like Christ, and isn't this the goal?

Yaconelli exclaims that, "Messy Spirituality is the description of the Christianity most of us live and that few of us admit." (p.16) In my call to transparency I risk vulnerability and share my brokenness in hope to testify that Jesus really loves despite past sin and failure. I have been humbled and struck down by my messy pride in denial that my life is and will always be under construction. Somehow in the midst of my testimonies of my past life I have claimed a false assertion that my life is tidy and neat, balanced and orderly. I agree with Yaconelli that instead my life is far from it. It is still unfinished, incomplete, and inexperienced.

***This poem was written when I thought I had it all together. While in therapy my psychologist became perplexed with each session as I changed my hair, my clothes, and even my mannerisms were different. It was during this time that I discovered that I was struggling with a potential multiple personality disorder.

Splitting

Tears rolled down my face
when my father died
I missed him so much
I was a dreamer with my dad
I realized in the midst of violent sobbing
when he died, I gave up
all the negative surrounded me
overwhelmed me
I lost belief
I lost hope
I can remember asking the Lord...
When did I lose my trust and you?
I was too young to accept
the death of my father
I became self-defeating
I became filled with worthlessness
I hid beneath my pain
I created other personas to justify
my integrity
"Syreena" was the first
the young innocent temptress
"Pamela" escaped
through the trials
and errors of Syreena
then you came Lord
and I became "Righteous Rita!"
sneaky righteous Rita

Angela never grew up
she screamed and closed the door
and died with her father Charles
now there is "Radiance"
she is the beginning and end
the eternal essence of all that
Angela ever dreamed of
all that Syreena,
Pamela,
and Rita
fought against
becoming

a new creature
Born for the second time

RAW SPIRIT

Yaconelli helps me sort out the reality of praying, "Thinking about God is being with God. Being with God is spirituality. Thinking about God is praying" (p.25). I think about God all the time. I used to think that I had to have a certain time and a certain place to pray. In some context I do believe that it is good for me to have a special place where I meet God in the mornings however, I <u>am</u> thinking about God all the time. This is affirmation to me that I do have an intimate connection with my Lord.

This is good.

Yaconelli uses the story of the Samaritan woman from the book of John to explore the ugliness of rejection. What is spiritually forming for me is to see how Jesus focused on this woman's <u>desire</u> for God. "Our search for love, for meaning, for happiness, is often our search for God in disguise" (p.59)

In the beginning of my spiritual journey I avoided Christians because I always expected condemnation and finger-pointing lectures. Even though I did not experience compassion, gentleness, kindness from my new church family. I experienced fear of being rejected and so I hid my secret sinful life and I only associated with Christians on Sundays. I never invited them over to my house because they might run into one of my male friends and that would have certainly been un-Christian. Yaconelli has given me the freedom to revisit my journals and discover that the Holy Spirit was working overtime with my desire for God.

You Were There

I was drowning
You with there Lord
reaching for my heart
I didn't see you
through all the disappointing love affairs
physical abuse
emotional fears
self affliction
self-destruction
You with there Lord
reaching for my hand
I couldn't see you
I was giving you just a little
and keeping the rest
for myself
Club on Saturday night
church on Sunday
unless I brought
someone home
then Monday was back
to self condemnation and guilt
by Tuesday I might
call for prayer
confession...
I thought about it
by Wednesday
my rationale was
winning
he called me
he loved me
he said
I was beautiful
I felt good again
being with me
that's all I needed
so by
Thursday the plan
was in motion
I'd spend Friday
deciding on the image
telling my girls
laughing about
how fine he was
I'd forgotten the
pain, the sin

Saturday I would rise
to the wardrobe
and plan my disguise
I was the master, you know
but you with there Lord
shielding me
hovering all around me
saving me from myself

as Saturday night came and went
Sunday morning
rang church bells
in my ears
each new day's sunshine
called me to my knees
until I finally
heard your voice
call out my name
my child, my child
come unto me
I will give you rest

ANGELA TAYLOR PERRY

I grew up as an only child for some years thinking I had no siblings.
When I was 13 the little girl I played with next door told me that her mother was my mother, too. What a shocking thing it was to find out that she was my sister!
As the years went by and I gained three _more_ sisters they became the people that I thought I needed acceptance from the most. When I was 14 I signed my own adoption papers to remain with my great aunt and uncle. I was afraid of my sister's father and I loved my great uncle. Consequently, I grew up as an only child.
My sisters labeled me as the strange and weird one. I was the black sheep, the odd one. I can relate with Yaconelli's words, "Oddness is a gift from God and sits dormant until God's Spirit gives it life and shape."
I thought that I needed to be like my sisters to be loved by them. It is _now_ wonderful to know that they do love me very deeply, just as I am. I praise God for spiritual mentors who helped me realize that oddness is a gift and
that God can use it for his glory.

The poem *"to be complete"* reflects my acceptance
of the *messy spirituality* of my life and that it is good for my life to be continuously under construction.

to be complete

God only knows what happened to me *in the fifties*
I remember my pet rooster, Folly
they cooked him
I remember little fair skinned Benny
we played barn doctor
I remember Aunt Doe Doe's creamed corn
it always tasted better than Granny's
I will always remember my father. . .
road the tractor with him
he was my buddy
In the sixties, President Kennedy was shot
love was everything
4-H, the dogs, and little white girls were my life
then I discovered sex
or rediscovered it
In the seventies, I went to college for three years
married twice
had three wonderful children
received Christ as the Lord
of my heart
and decided not to go into prostitution
good choice!

In the eighties, I had three back surgeries
married one more fruitless time
experienced entrepreneurship
weathered the storms of physical abuse
broke my left ankle,
and was diagnosed
with multiple sclerosis
then I got stronger
So far *in the nineties*,
I've met my real father
broke my right ankle
had a hysterectomy
decided what I want to be when I grow up
learned to love a <u>real</u> good man
and
to be continued. . .

Search me

Search me, O God, and know my heart;
test me and know my anxious thoughts. See if there be any offensive way in me and lead me in the way everlasting. (Psalm 139:23,24)

I have made the circle from depending on You
to depending on myself, again.

This time I realize that You are listening to me.
In times past I would not have stopped in my sin and said Search me...
I would have kept on sinning until I hated myself again.
But I don't hate myself, I love myself. You **are** teaching me. Thank you for opening my heart and thank you for this time of communion

Search me, O God
I worship you O God
In the sanctuary of my soul
This earthen vessel
So unworthy, so wretched
Comes before your holy presence
Bows down before you
Waits...
Thank you Jesus! Hallelujah
You are holy, you are mighty
King of kings and Lord of Lord's

I worship you this morning
In my spirit
My spirit longs for union with you—once again
I stand firm against the flesh in its will to renounce itself above Spirit
The flesh has no power
I confess the evil of my flesh and its will to take over my mind
I am yours Lord Hallelujah
I want to glorify you
You only
You are my redeemer
You are my wisdom
You are my peace
You are my joy
You are my gladness
You are beauty
You are strength
Thank you Jesus!!!!
For loving me
For wanting me
When I'm so unlovely

RAW SPIRIT

I confess my sin my unforgiveness
My stubbornness
My empty will, it has no substance—
It's just empty space, empty words
It says –stay in the bed
Don't get up—don't commune
With spirit—Spirit can't help
Stay here—you need more rest
It's not time to rise
Stay here—
Empty, empty words
No substance moving me to sin
Moving me to nothingness my will rejoices in iniquity
Rejoices in my guilt
But you saved me this morning lord
You said get up now! Before it's too late
And my will in that split second says, "rest"
Spirit says, 'sit up, put one foot on the floor and the other will follow
Hear me I am calling you
I want to sit with you, **My Child**
Revive you
Be your everything, fill your cup, until it runs over with joy
Thank you Jesus
O thank you father
I love you, I love me
You have saved me, again
From this wretched self that I am
You are wisdom
You are humility
You are justice
You are temperance
Thou hath not given me a spirit of fear
A spirit of doubt
A spirit of procrastination
Thou hath not given me
Lack of esteem lack of worth
Thou hath given me
Love and power and discipline
Thou hath not given me a spirit of fear
But one of power and love and self control
Thank you Jesus
O thank you Thank ya!
Glory be to your name
This moment Hallelujah in my spirit
Hallelujah in my inner sanctuary
You are my strength and I worship you
You are my refreshment
And I worship you

ANGELA TAYLOR PERRY

You are my hope and I praise you
You are my faith and I worship you
You are sweetness you are beauty
You are my eternal life
You are great omnipotent merciful savior
I love you lord
I love you!
Thank you for drawing me near unto you this morning
How could I lay in bed wide awake in contentment?
My soul cried out
You called me
Here I am lord
Use me up, today
Teach me your wisdom
Teach me your gladness
Teach me your courage
I breathe in your comfort
Help me praise you
Come Holy Spirit
My mind is yours
I love you Lord
O How I love you
Ty ty ty ty ty ty Jesus
Ty ty ty ty ty ty O Glory!
I present my body as a living sacrifice
I worship you o father
In my spirit
In my mind
In my heart
In my soul
In my sanctuary
With my eyes
I worship you O God
With my feet
With my hands
With my ears
With my fingers
What ever I look upon O God
My eyes glorify you O God
Whatever I listen to
O God
May my hearing glorify you
Whatever my thoughts are O God
May my thinking glorify you
I offer my body as a living sacrifice
A constant dedication of my body moment by moment
I will humbly offer this wretched flesh unto thee
I dedicate my body

RAW SPIRIT

So that I might live for you and keep on living for you
I offer my body as a living sacrifice wherever I am
Where ever I go
I don't need a special time
A special place
A special hour
I offer my body, Right now!
While my body is living and while my flesh is warring.
Yes Lord! This is it
Guide my prayers O God
I am in Holy Communion with You
Guide me to the inner sanctuary of my soul

I worship you O God
You are so mighty
So blessed
So complete
You are hope
Hallelujah! Glory be to your name
I love you, I love you
I offer my body as a living sacrifice
I sacrifice my flesh
All my desires
All my passions
All my pleasures
I will not pollute my body with the sins of this world.
I stand firm in spirit against fulfilling my flesh and its appetite
In every way
What I look at
What I listen to
What I say
What I touch
Where I go
I submit my flesh to you and offer it as a living sacrifice

On Prayer, Meditation, Monastic Silence Community

Augustine: "Everywhere the greater joy is ushered in by the greater pain". (p.41)

James 1:2 exclaims that we must count it all joy when we go through trials and temptations...

What a challenge! It is my belief that if we can give God but one ounce of a chance to shine through our pain He will give us patience and hope. It is not easy being a 'triumphant survivor of Multiple Sclerosis and Spondylolithesis' however the Christian life is not promised to be easy. We are promised joy but I know too well that it takes some longsuffering to just catch a glimpse of what this joy might look like.

John of the Cross: from stanzas of the soul that suffers with longing to see God

This love I sense that this man had for God is breath taking to me. The line "I am dying because I do not die" is profound in my heart because in all that he expresses, he experiences no real joy or comfort because he is alive. Dieing is freedom and the ultimate spiritual space. Personally, I can see how this might be reached through prayer and meditation in the monastic community away from worldly distractions. I have often longed to experience this. The closest I come to it is in my early morning times alone with God before the house awakes.

John Wesley— speaks of "observing the Wednesday and Friday Fasts commonly observed in the ancient Church: tasting no food till three in the afternoon."

The discipline of fasting has become known to me as a devout order of personal worship and practice of offering my body as a <u>living sacrifice</u>. This discipline teaches that God is near which draws me to become spiritually acute in my listening to God's voice. My husband and I practice a 24 to 36 hour fast once a week on Monday's. We maintain our traditional five day fast between Christmas and the New Year. We use the actual holiday as preparation for the fast rather than plunging into food. We have talked of going to the The Hermitage to experience an environment of attentiveness to God for this five day period. This will be a big leap, yet one that we look forward to with great spiritual ecstasy.

a period of purification

I present my body as a living sacrifice
I accept your direction to first deny my body its natural appetites:
To wage the war of my flesh
To render my body a fitter instrument of purity and more obedient
To the good notions of divine grace
To dry up the springs of my passions that war against my soul

This time of purification
O God
Grant me spiritual insight
Into the chains that bind me and the courage to throw them off.
Show me my prison and show me the way out.
Identify ambiguous relationships and ambivalent attitudes.
I will identify and choose
righteousness.

I will come to you even when I don't feel like it.
I will come and sit with you and pray and wait for your voice
I will pray with others.
I will pray in church.
I will pray alone with you.
I will not be afraid.
Lord, give me your courage, your strength

Let me see myself in the light of your mercy and choose You.
Amen

ANGELA TAYLOR PERRY

Thomas Merton— His constant inner torment is worth a measure of personal devotion. He shares evidence of the Spirit speaking to him from the Word. I find that I have an affinity with his spiritual connection for I too have experienced the Word become flesh to me in the words "**The spirit of the Lord is upon me**" (Isaiah 61:1). When first these words illumined my heart a song burst forth and remains a tune that I sing to acknowledge the presence of the Holy Spirit. This scripture sooths my inner agony and despair with God's comfort and I am encouraged to continue to *press on for the mark for the prize of the high calling of God in Christ Jesus.*

Merton again: "It seemed that every step I took carried me painfully forward under a burden of desires that almost crushed me with the monotony of their threat, the searching familiarity of their ever-present disgust." The image 'under a burden of desires' is so vivid to me, like an umbrella weighted down with all of my lures and temptations just a hand stretch away. The flesh wants to be satisfied and the spirit wars against the momentary distracting indulgence. This is what helps me to make the righteous choice—the fact that to satisfy a desire is only achieved for a moment and then spiritually I am practically starting all over."

Merton and Yaconelli affirm of God's grace and profess that I must stop trying to be perfect! And I must stop telling myself that since I am not perfect I can't be loved.

On Charismatic Gifts, Visions, Revelations, Miracles, and the Call to Ministry

Julian of Norwich:— I would like to comment on her first and second graces that she desired of God. The first was to have recollection of Christ's passion.

I wanted to experience this also and so I went to see the "Passion of Christ" movie three times. Each time I went so that I might experience his passion and his love for the Father and all who denied him. Awesome! I went three times and after the third, the Spirit said it was enough. Each time I was filled with so much joy I could hardly contain its fullness in my body and soul. I was one in the spirit even with the actor for I know he had a great spiritual awakening.

Her second desire was for bodily sickness and the degree of her request as quoted here, "in this sickness I wanted to have every kind of pain, bodily and spiritual which I should have if I were dying, every fear and assault from devils, and every other kind of pain …"

This seems unimaginable and undesirable limited by our limited minds. Yet, through my own walk with pain and adversity I believe that this kind of endurance and call is truly a gift. I believe that God gives some an extra measure of his sovereign grace to endure and count the cost for Christ to give Him Glory. It is a miracle for me to have endured and it frightens me to think that I will have to endure more but I know that God will take me through it and He will *smile* and for that I wait with great hope.

Confidence in Him

"As the father has loved me, so have I loved you, continue ye in my love. If you keep my commandments, you still abide in my love, even as I have kept my father's commandments, and abide in His love. These things I have spoken unto you, that my Joy might remain in you, and that your joy might be full."
John 15: 9-11

During the first year of the beginning of my spiritual journey in knowing the Lord, I used to wonder how I could sustain the fleeting moments of inner joy and peace I was experiencing deep in my soul. Not long after my divorce from my first husband, I became very reclusive and depressed. All I wanted was peace of mind. My mind seemed tormented by fear, doubts, and disappointment. I longed for companionship. I kept the house dark, and slept a lot. My new friends at Church invited me to go to a retreat. My spirit was lifted as I listened to the speaker share her testimony of God's love in her life. I wanted what she had and I knew that day that I would be standing in front of others, sharing my life and being an encourager. That was 15 years before God began to fulfill His vision for my life.

The journey towards holiness is a process and is not complete until the day of the Lord's coming. When the woman finished her talk that day, she concluded by asking if anyone had any questions. There were many. She had blessed everyone's heart quite deeply. It seemed I had my hand up forever waiting to ask my question. I felt an urgency to be patient. I knew God had something special for me to know through this woman. I asked, "Sometimes I feel that I have so much joy inside, and other times I feel just the opposite. What can I do to maintain peace of mind?" I spoke quickly out of fear. I didn't want the other women to know too much about me. The church thing was a new experience for me and this retreat was too much disclosure. Little did I know that in the years to come, that's exactly what I would be doing; sharing the intimacies of my life and risking vulnerability to encourage other women to be free and complete in Christ! The answers the woman gave me are found in *John 15:9-11*. That's it! Every question she was asked, she answered with a scripture. I remember thinking; I want to know the Bible like that. It was amazing and foreign to me that I had this desire. Prior to this, my desire in literature was elicit romance novels. Reading scripture was difficult to grasp. Truthfully, it took a number of years before God gave me revelation knowledge as to the deep meaning He had for me in His precious word. Love was all I desired. Love and more love. I was so lonely. The word in John 15 said, *"If you keep my commandments and abide in my love."* This meant when I keep His commandments, I am abiding in His love. My being obedient to His words would grant me the peace my soul earnestly desired. When this reality hit me, it knocked me down! Obedience meant I had a lot of work to do and I wasn't completely ready to let go of everything. I knew I had to. As time went on, I learned God's mercy. His mercy is everlasting. His forgiveness is inconceivable and His grace is without a doubt, sufficient.

"If we confess our sins, He is faithful and just to forgive us our sins and to cleanse us from all unrighteousness." I John 1.9

My confidence comes in knowing that God loves me just like I am.
Just like He created me.

RAW SPIRIT

I Am

the day I became a swan
I stretched wide
my wings
arched my long willowy neck
and with my feet
firm on the ground
I made my statement
and said
I too
am a
Beautiful Black Queen
now
I can fly!

On Service, Self-disciplines, and the Active Life

Parker Palmer—a quote from his book *Let Your Life Speak* (Yaconelli, p.73)

"Vocation does not mean a goal that I pursue. It means a calling that I hear. Before I can tell my life what I want to do with it, I must listen to my life telling me who I am"

Isn't that backwards for Western thinking? From the time we are little we are asked well "What do you want to be when you grow up?" Maybe they can see that you are artistic or maybe good at fixing things or compassionate with children, but do they encourage you in who you are?

As a Christian this becomes an effervescent reality. The question to ask is who am I? What are my passions? What am I good at? In what areas is my life effective and fruit-bearing? Once this is fine tuned then it's just about refinement by letting

God do his thing.

It took me a while to get this through my skull. I struggled for years about which area I should choose: singing, writing, speaking, and now art. I was a *perplexed sister* for a long time.

My direction is <u>now</u> coming from my seminary/mentor professors.

God is using them in particular ways to open my eyes to what has always been.

Glory Hallelujah!

Echoes of a Voice

Oh what an experience
I feel cheated of my blackness
I feel anger
ENVY
almost hate for the white in me
I want to holler at my mother
she was doing her best
Her best
but not my best
what was best?
I am angry because I can see the Black in me
I can't feel the Black in me
and to think that one time
I took pride in not sounding Black
now my heart bleeds to be free of this
White façade
all her faces
Will the real me stand up!
Stand up and be counted among the rest
not set apart, labeled
for what
My ego is not vain
only my pride
but which one
the Black or the White?
my heart cries out to my many
brothers and sisters
who were forced in their ignorance
to become somebody
but who
We are not White or are we?
We look Black, we sound white
we look
out of Black faces through white perspectives
Somewhere deep in our souls we find the rhythm
We hear the drum
We rock on the beat
Yet something is missing
Something that doesn't allow us to fit
Black or white
so who the hell are we?
help us... we hurt

ANGELA TAYLOR PERRY

My seminary experience taught me that being African American
is part of my definition. (And this is not always obvious)
I realize that I don't have to hide behind a white façade for fear of rejection.
Instead I have learned to bring my colorful, multifaceted heritage to a higher dimension. During my clinical
pastoral care experience I became confident within myself through group affirmation by being willing to
watch how people perceived me.
As I learned how to mirror people through active listening, I connected with each one from their
perspective instead of mine. This was important to my pastoral identity.

Being Born for the Third Time

I do not remember being born the first time
I can only imagine what it might have been like
my mother in labor—the pain—the time
traveling down the birth canal
Only to be exposed
I do remember being born for the second time
it was painful realizing I was a sinner
it was laborious accepting God's forgiveness
forgiving myself
exposed again
now here I sit
in wonder and amazement!
I made it through
after ten weeks of labor
ten weeks of disclosure
ten weeks of discovering my weaknesses
broken again
before God
Yet this time not alone
this time surrounded by other wounded babes
crying out together, praising God for being chosen
to be
Born for the third time

ANGELA TAYLOR PERRY

*What does it mean to be an African American woman
in the Christian Reformed Church?*

I believe it means change!

The question I asked myself was what I bring to the table of a denomination characterized by some with rigidity, lack of emotion, cold compassion, and segregation. In this 21st century, as a 52-year-old black woman who grew up ignorant to the depth of White privilege and Black oppression. I walk and live in a so-called free world. Where there are laws against discriminating against race, gender, age, and disability. I live in a country that was once built on Christian principles that takes pride in its efforts to alleviate oppression and poverty abroad, yet struggles with people of like circumstances here at home. Where do I fit in the great historical continuum with women like Harriet Tubman, Sojourner Truth, Rosa Parks, and Oprah Winfrey? What do I bring to the table of church folk that asks me, "Well, what brought **you** to Calvin seminary?"

After reading two books: *"Daughters of Thunder"* and *"For such a time as this..."*;

I can no longer answer this question with "Well, my church membership is at Immanuel CRC in Kalamazoo; or the years of singing in CRC churches brought me here, or the times I have spoken at CRC ladies luncheons, or that my kids attended Christian schools... I can no longer identify my exposure to the Christian Reformed Church with patronizing answers that seem only to relax my interviewer. These two quotes, first from a White and then from a Black Women have been pensive thoughts for me to explore.

"For such a time as this", edited by Lillian V. Grissen:

"The thread that ties the stories together is not first of all the accomplishments of these women but rather their use of God-given gifts...... Reformed theology emphasizes that Christians fill a threefold office: prophet, priest, and king (or should we say prophetess, priestess, and Queen?). In a conference paper entitled "Tasks of a prophetic church" (Orbis, 1982) Jacqueline Grant has identified a prophet in part as a Christian who has the ability to discern the will of God for her life, who stands for justice and transformation, who is not afraid to confront evil, and who seeks to build a community of faith, partnership, justice, and unity."

"I will pour out my spirit all in all people

your sons and daughters will prophesy..." Acts 2:17

"Daughters of Thunder" by Bettye Collier-Thomas:

"Acknowledgment of the significance of African American women and Black religious history is one of the most prominent advances in recent African American scholarship. The study of Black women and religion is crucial to our understanding of American and Black religion. A focus on Black churchwomen's experiences changes the nature of African American history and introduces new dimensions to the discourse on religious tradition and authority, which have been traditionally defined as male history."

RAW SPIRIT

On Pastoral Formation

Revelation

it amazes me how one moment one can be high in the spirit
happy in the Lord
praising his name for all the good things he has done
preparing to tell others
how wonderful he is
how blessed you are
and then in the quickest moment the circumstance changes
today
after a humbling time with a sister in Christ
receiving God's grace
praying with her
laughing with her
rejoicing with her
thankful for God's faithfulness
after parting
still glowing in His power by His strength
excited about today and ready to serve him
and then
I fell
I was walking rather briskly
feeling confident in my stride
feeling victorious about the absence of MS
but it is not absent
how do I do this? Why do I walk so happy and forget so quickly?
my foot, my toe caught what seemed like the floor rising
all who suffer with this disease know this cute symptom
I had prepared devotion for a small group
I had prepared to share with them God's grace through suffering
God's grace through our weaknesses, through our misfortunes and infirmities
I was ready to take them to the foot of the cross
and weep with them as they were comforted
by his grace
I sit here **Angry**!
Angryangryangryangry
disappointed, unhappy, questioning, worrying, fighting anxiety,
wondering why?
feeling not ready for advanced suffering
not ready for another transition-- a new pain, a new disorder
a new fight
I listen to my body...
waiting for it to cry out to me its limitation
a sorrow
its need for care
and I think I can't do this
I can't keep going on like this

I don't want to
I Scream!!!!!!
I can't believe you want me to help people with suffering when I'm suffering
How, how do I do this?
you say ---I must trust God to deliver me through whatever suffering afflicts me
no matter the severity...
why?
you say-- **you must realize the suffering teaches you that you are not self-sufficient**
I am not self-sufficient
It is by grace
through my weakness
that I am strong
I know this
I was going to preach <u>this</u>
this morning
now here I sit angry
in pain and in fear
of what may lie ahead
"if so be that we suffer with him, that we may be also glorified together"
Romans 8:17

RAW SPIRIT

"if there be therefore any consolation in Christ,
if any comfort of love
if any fellowship of the spirit
if any bowels and mercies,
fulfill ye my joy
then be ye like-minded,
having the same love,
being of one accord,
of one mind" Phil. 2:1,2
"for this light affliction,
which is but for a moment,
works for us
of far more exceeding and eternal weight
of glory;
while we look not at the things which are seen
but at the things which are not seen: for the things which are seen
are temporal;
but the things which are not seen
are eternal 2cor.4:17-18
there it is
faith is the substance of things hoped for
and the evidence of things not seen
maybe the courage to endure suffering
is the thing hoped for
and the grace of God
his magnificent eternal power at work
through weakness is
evidence that God is real unseen—

ANGELA TAYLOR PERRY

As a baby Christian I learned how to trust in God for all the consequences of my sinful life through daily devotion's of confession and prayer.
The poem "Revelation", written in my seventh week of pastoral internship expresses my trusting through suffering. Many people are puzzled as to how I define Multiple Sclerosis as a 'gift'. MS transformed my life, my children's life, and all those in my immediate circle. I have asked my children, "What would you do if you had MS?" At age 19, my middle son answered, "I'd be just like you Mom". I was in awe.
They say they would be sad, but not for long because they know how to fight.
These words from my children continue to bless me.
Being adopted and growing up longing for family has become fulfilled in my passion to bring people together in the unity of Christ's love.

Koinonia Love
Acts 2:42-47

Wonder

I wonder sometime
what would my life have been like
if I had made different choices
if I had not sat in the sand
eating stone ground marbles at the age two
if I had not played barn doctor
with little fair skinned Benny at seven
moved to the big house
got my period at eleven
I wonder sometime
what would my life be like
if I hadn't winked, blinked, and romanticized
a man in prison at age thirteen
if I had not let my high school sweetheart climb
in the window and steel my virginity at fifteen
I wonder sometime
what would my life be like
if I had not gone to college at seventeen
and believed every fool man
that said I was beautiful
could be trusted like my dad
followed them, drank with them, laughed with them
I wonder sometime
what would my life be like today
if that one had not drugged me
raped me
and left me without hope at eighteen

Then I got married
O how scary
One, two, three times, now four
I said I do
three times life sprung from my womb
three times life died in my womb
three times my body succumbed to a surgeons knife

I wonder sometime
what would my life be like today
if I had made different choices
if I had decided to sell my body

but I didn't
I made different choices
righteous choices
I am blessed to be a part of the healing

of some of my regrets
I am blessed to be set free from cigarettes
I am blessed to be set free from
addictions, afflictions, seductions
insinuations, accusations, temptations
hallelujah!

I wonder sometime
what would my life be like today
if Jesus had condemned me
rejected me, and left me
instead he freed me
released me
instead he saved me

The Music of Grace

—plays righteous notes
not wrong notes
The music of grace plays the base
deep in forgiveness
and high with mercy
The stringed instruments pulsate joy throughout the soul
and soothe the tired weary mind
a mind who has given in to waste and want
but continues to thirst
no longer does pleasure satisfy the longing
no longer does the heart seek itself
for when the heart of the sinner sees the Glory of God
she is set free from bondage
the chains of addiction are broken
rebellion has ceased
The music of grace bursts forth from the heart
In a new movement
sin is only a parasite
Only a vandal, only spoiler
The music of grace is enchanted with
sin
for without sin
there would be no need
for
grace

ANGELA TAYLOR PERRY

Ending On a Reformed Note

After four years of seminary the most liberating accent that I now possess knows that I don't have to stop being African American in order to be reformed. This may seem obvious to many in the majority culture, it is a message that for me, needs to be understood theologically and clearly in order for me to articulate the reason I believe I am called to the Christian Reformed Church. I came to seminary as a singer/poet and now a liturgical artist. On the day my professor explored ways in which I could integrate my art into my ministry was the day a huge piece of the puzzle of my life was found.

Exploring other writer's spiritual journeys is a formative way to know God deeper and personally and also helps round out the intellectual academic experience. In other words, reading life stories is getting real with God; getting to the heart.

As an African American Christian I see my experience and existence as being ordained by God, according to his plan and for his glory. I am excited about expressing this through preaching, music and art within a reformed theological worldview. I embrace reformed theology because it aligns with everything that the African American church has sought to be: biblical, historical, and experiential.

The African American church holds the Bible in the highest regard. The Bible has always been the center of the Black community as well as church life. In light of this, the Reformed commitment to the Bible as the primary source of truth and authority should find a warm welcome in African American Christianity. I accept the challenge to all my culturally diverse brothers and sisters to exhibit this reality.

From a historical perspective, if anything distinguishes the African American Church, it is its insistence on remembering and honoring those who have gone before. This insistence does not stand alone and is right at home in Reformed theology. I have come to embrace that Reformed theology understands that while we are always seeking new expressions of the truth, we are not seeking new truth.

From an experiential perspective, the life of the African American church has not been one of just talking about the faith but also of living out that faith. African American preaching though sometimes vibrant and repetitious rarely goes without practical application. Life was never to be understood apart from the knowledge of God. I have learned that Reformed theology is experiential. It helps us see the reality and the experience of humans in their relationship with each other and with God.

CPSIA information can be obtained
at www.ICGtesting.com
Printed in the USA
LVIC04n2301030416
482019LV00005B/24